ideals®
MOTHER'S DAY
2005

Dedicated to a celebration of the American ideals of faith in God, loyalty to country, and love of family.

Features

Departments

Cover: Lavender and purple hydrangeas drape gracefully over a fence next to a cottage in Cannon Beach, Oregon. Photograph by Steve Terrill.

Inside Front Cover: Roses, the most elegant of flowers, make a beautiful arrangement in this painting entitled A STILL LIFE OF ROSES, *by Frans Mortelmans (1865-1936). Image from Fine Art Photographic Library, Ltd., London/Galerie Mensing.*

IDEALS—Vol. 62, No. 2, March 2005 IDEALS (ISSN 0019-137X, USPS 256-240) is published six times a year: January, March, May, July, September, and November by IDEALS PUBLICATIONS, a division of Guideposts, 39 Seminary Hill Road, Carmel, NY 10512. Copyright © 2005 by IDEALS PUBLICATIONS, a division of Guideposts. All rights reserved. The cover and entire contents of IDEALS are fully protected by copyright and must not be reproduced in any manner whatsoever. Title IDEALS registered U.S. Patent Office. Printed and bound in USA. Printed on Weyerhaeuser Husky. The paper used in this publication meets the minimum requirements of American National Standard for Information Sciences—Permanence of Paper for Printed Library Materials, ANSI Z39.48-1984. Periodicals postage paid at Carmel, New York, and additional mailing offices. Canadian mailed under Publications Mail Agreement Number 40010140. POSTMASTER: Send address changes to IDEALS, 39 Seminary Hill Road, Carmel, NY 10512. CANADA POST: Send address changes to Guideposts PO Box 1051, Fort Erie ON L2A 6C7. For subscription or customer service questions, contact IDEALS Publications, a division of Guideposts, 39 Seminary Hill Road, Carmel, NY 10512. Fax 845-228-2115. Reader Preference Service: We occasionally make our mailing lists available to other companies whose products or services might interest you. If you prefer not to be included, please write to IDEALS Customer Service.

ISBN 0-8249-1301-9   GST 893989236

Visit the IDEALS website
at www.idealsbooks.com

Morning's Touch

Helen Ann Heath

Let a morning softly touch you;
Feel its coolness on your face.
Let it silently enfold you
In its gentle, sweet embrace.

Feel the magic of the moment
With your heart, your soul, your mind;
Experience serenity
In the beauty you will find.

Reach out and touch a rosebud
With its blossom fresh and new.

Caress the velvet softness
While it's wet with morning dew.

Grasp the golden sunlight
And the breeze, so mild and meek,
As they both emerge in splendor
To brush against your cheek.

Gently touch the natural beauty
Before it is transposed;
Feel the grace of early morn
While the dew is on the rose.

A Morning Prayer

Ella Wheeler Wilcox

Let me today do something that will take
    A little sadness from the world's vast store,
And may I be so favored as to make
    Of joy's too scanty sum a little more.

Let me not hurt, by any selfish deed
    Or thoughtless word, the heart of foe or friend.
Nor would I pass unseeing worthy need,
    Or sin by silence when I should defend.

However meager be my worldly wealth,
    Let me give something that shall aid my kind—
A word of courage, or a thought of health
    Dropped as I pass for troubled hearts to find.

Let me tonight look back across the span
    'Twixt dawn and dark and to my conscience say—
Because of some good act to beast or man,
    "The world is better that I lived today."

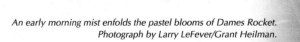

An early morning mist enfolds the pastel blooms of Dames Rocket.
Photograph by Larry LeFever/Grant Heilman.

The Sun's Kiss

Georgia B. Adams

The lilacs here in clusters hang
Where, softly, winds just blew;
All purple-hued, their graceful heads
Are moist with morning dew.
The fragrance of this hour is
The touch of the Divine.
Just for this little span of time
The moment's mine, all mine.
I know a peace of heart
Here, now, amid all this,
As the sun o'er lilacs stops
To share a morning kiss.

Before the Day Begins

Nova Trimble Ashley

Some mornings I must get away,
Away from living's din,
And so I rise at break of day
To watch the day begin.
I stand beneath the maple tree
And touch its emerald lace,
Or I may spot a bumblebee
Intent on saying grace.
Sometimes I hear a tiny wren,
Its song just pouring out.
I smell the roses too; and, then,
I pause or walk about
Till suddenly my life is whole.
I am ready, come what may.
This morning I must feed my soul
Before I start the day.

The hues of a pink and red tea rose are beautifully highlighted by the violet blossoms of Double Delight larkspur. Photograph by Jessie Walker.

COUNTRY CHRONICLE

Lansing Christman

ON A MAY MORNING

May is a time of singing, a time of blossom and flower, green grass, and pageantry across the hills. Flowers burst into bloom, one after another, adding their colorful hues to the beauty of the land.

How inspiring these days are. Look closely at the dew-covered grass of morning when the sun comes. Each sprout and spire wears its pearl-like jewels, sparkling in the light of a new day.

Beauty and song can be found at every turn, for May is filled with the rhythm of spring's flowing ways. I feel intensely the warmth of the lengthening sunlight as it brings renewed life to field and meadow, to pasture and woodland.

May's smoothing touch is everywhere in flower-strewn paths and in singing streams. And I listen to the songs of birds, the daytime songs and those that fill the hours of stars.

I always step quietly as I walk through a lane of song that comes from tree and hedge and thicket in the hills and valley lands. Each carol and trill, each warble and melody, add to the glorious symphony of the year.

But on this Mother's Day morning, there is a special song I want to hear: I want to listen to the moving, whistled song of the white-throated sparrow. It is a song that tugs at my heart and opens the gate to my garden of memories.

The author of four books, Lansing Christman has contributed to IDEALS for more than thirty years. Mr. Christman has also been published in several American, international, and braille anthologies. He lives in rural South Carolina.

What better way to spend a warm afternoon than by walking through a meadow blooming with wildflowers, as depicted in this painting by Caroline Emilie Mundt (1842-1922). Image from Fine Art Photographic Library, Ltd., London/Waterhouse & Dodd.

The Lilac
Humbert Wolfe

Who thought of the lilac?
"I," dew said,
"I made up the lilac,
out of my head."

"She made up the lilac!
Pooh!" thrilled a linnet,
and each dew-note had a
lilac in it.

Let Me
Come Back
Cecil L. Gatten

Let me come back in lilac time,
No matter where I roam;
Wherever I am at lilac time,
I long again for home.
Though other fields may greener be
And sunnier be the clime,
Old memories will return to me
When comes sweet lilac time.

Purple lilac blooms bend gracefully with the gentle breezes of a garden in Bristol, New Hampshire. Photograph by William H. Johnson.

BACKYARD CALENDAR

Joan Donaldson

Although the wind is brisk, a weathered board fence shelters me as I weed rows of spinach, beets, and lettuce in my small garden. Pea vines, sporting tiny pods, spiral upward across black netting. These vegetables required the cool soils of early spring to germinate, but now soft rains and longer, sun-filled days have warmed the tilled beds. A variety of fresh green plants flourishes within my garden, and each passing day reveals subtle changes. The promise of renewal has begun, like the swelling of buds on my heirloom roses that border the garden fence.

Tender shoots sprout at the bases of the roses. Although these canes are filled with the youthful energy of the season, they yet require a bit of guidance. I prune away dead wood to create space for the new life. Snipping twine, I tie one end to a board and thread it around the rose canes, lifting them close to the fence. Spring days encourage tidying up, both of this garden and my life.

Now, more than on New Year's Day, I find myself making resolutions and seeking change. This is a season of vigor, a time to cut away sloth or nagging worries, and to participate in this regeneration of the natural world. I move along the border of roses, tying up each plant while I admire their feathery new leaves.

I weave the supple branches of the Seven Sisters through the small sections of lath that arches over my garden gate. For years, I photographed my sons under this arch. When my husband and I adopted them, their heads did not reach halfway up the fence. Now, after eighteen springs, they must duck in order to avoid the dangling branches.

While I plant crops for my family, the whir of wings fills the air around me as chickadees and tufted titmice seek food for their recently hatched broods. I shed my jacket and fill my garden cart with compost. The rich scent of humus and compost mingle as I methodically dig holes along a marked row. I set in tomato plants, slip on a tin collar to protect them, and mulch with compost. This instant row of greenery celebrates the revival taking placing during these final

Now, more than on New Year's Day, I find myself making resolutions and seeking change.

weeks in May. Wool coats and muddy boots have been relegated to the backroom. The fear of frost has dwindled as spring marches towards June.

Now I scan the sky for thunderheads. If a storm were to come through, it could blow winds that could flatten infant plants; and sudden cloudbursts could send gushing rivers across my weeded beds. But the softness of the evening shows no threat of storms and reminds me that soon I will walk barefoot down these garden paths.

In the strawberry bed dotted with white blos-

soms, young leaves cover the remains of last year's foliage. A few runners creep out onto the paths. In a few short weeks, red berries will hide beneath these leaves. Beside those beds, corn will send tassels skywards, and gray-green squash vines will creep between the rows.

Gardeners are perennial optimists. With a fistful of seed packets, we plant with faith, weed with fury, and watch as the scene we envisioned unfolds. We labor with the mindset that this season will be the best ever.

Before heading inside, I pause to pick up my basket of seeds that I left beneath a stocky Scottish rose. Dozens of ivory-tipped buds sparkle among the leaves. In the warmth of the morning, one has begun to unfold and reveals petals still cupped like seashells. Like this beautiful small blossom, each day of spring brings new joys and pleasures. I breathe in the scent of roses and delight in the transformation spreading across my backyard sanctuary.

Joan Donaldson is the author of a picture book and a young adult novel, as well as essays that have appeared in many national publications. She and her husband raised their sons on Pleasant Hill Farm in Michigan, where they continue to practice rural skills.

Talisman
Ruth Jenner

God took soft flakes of sunset sky
And dipped them in the moonlight's gold,
Wrapped them in fluted leaves to dry,
Then watched their loveliness unfold.
And thus, nudged by spring's warmth, there grows,
With fragrant petals gently curled,
This sunset-tinted, moon-gilt rose
That God designed and gave the world.

Song of the Rose
Mrs. Roy Cole

No beautiful palace have I on the hill,
No pictures to hang in my halls;
But never a painter could match with his skill
The roses abloom on my walls.
When down my green valley in purple and gold
The morning comes dewy and bright,
I look from my window to see them unfold
Their buds at the kiss of the light.
And when at the evening my labor is o'er
And shadows grow long on the lea,
The sweet breath of roses floats in at the door,
As if each had grown just for me.

Roses in the Pasture
Freda Newton Bunner

All small and sweet pink they lie
Upon the pasture's breast,
Their only task to please a thrush
Or hide a rabbit's nest.
And all they ask is song and sun
And night's cool charity;
And all their lives are beautiful,
Though no one comes to see.

*Roses, calla lilies, and ivy make a fanciful
centerpiece built around a white birdcage.
Photograph by Jessie Walker.*

The Wild Rose

Irene Wilson

Of a Spider

Wilfrid Thorley

The spider weaves his silver wire
Between the cherry and the brier.

He runs along and sees the thread
Well-fastened on each hawser-head.

And then within his wheel he dozes,
Hung on a thorny stem of roses,

While fairies ride the silver ferry
Between the rosebud and the cherry.

I know a place where loveliness grows—
I often wander there,
Where the wild rose lifts its pale pink face
To the sunshine's friendly stare.

And when, in the cool of the evening,
Its petals are wet with dew,
There is nothing to me more enchanting
Than this flower of exquisite hue.

Oh, pity the poor foolish people
Who are so busy they miss
The sight of this delicate blossom
That the bees and the butterflies kiss.

*A pasture rose blooms near Ham Brook in Franconia,
New Hampshire. Photograph by William H. Johnson.*

An Old Fashioned Mother
Louise Lamica

She was wise, but not as the world measures wisdom. She had a firm conviction that May rain would do no harm, that melted snow saved from March would heal a burn, and that a wish made on a new moon would come true.

Her wisdom was reflected in the flowers that bloomed bountifully under her care, in a garden that flourished near a cool forest glen. Her wisdom was hidden in the tenderness of her touch, the trust she put in her loved ones, and in the sweetness of our home.

She was simple, as the world measures simplicity. But I would not have had her otherwise, the woman I knew as Mother.

To a Lovely Lady
Jessie Terry Olcott

One day from your garden
You gave me a rose.
The joy that it gave me
Only I know.
You gave me back part
Of a life I had known:
Sweet memories of gardens,
Of Mother at home
Snipping white double roses
To make a bouquet
For wayfarers like me
Who were passing that way.

Beauty of White House Grounds
Theodore Roosevelt

The grounds are too lovely for anything, and spring is here, or rather early summer, in full force. Mother's flower gardens are now as beautiful as possible, and the iron railings of the fences south of them are covered with clematis and roses in bloom. The trees are in full foliage and the grass brilliant green, and my friends, the warblers, are trooping to the north in full force.

A climbing rose provides a canopy for a garden overflowing with eye-catching blossoms. Photograph by D. Petku/H. Armstrong Roberts.

READERS' REFLECTIONS

My Garden
Marjorie W. Beach
FallsChurch, Virginia

As I walk in my garden and from the world retreat,
Surrounded by His handiwork, His presence with me meets.
I thank Him for my flowers in their many varied hues;
For the glistening on their leaves of early morning dew;
For the fragrance of the lily, the lilac and the rose;
For the whippoorwill's call at twilight when morning glories close,
For the moonlight's reflection on the pebbled paths at night,
I thank my Lord and Savior, my precious Guiding Light.

Blossoms
Cassandra Fleming
Sanford, Florida

Just as flowers in a garden are watered from above,
So a child's heart is watered with a mother's gentle love.
You've cared for me for many years
With love so tenderly;
Keep watering me faithfully—
A blossom you soon will see.

Gifts from God
Amy L. Jump
Alexander, Iowa

We get a glimpse of heaven,
From the beauties that we see,
Such wonders as the sunrise,
Or a tall and graceful tree,

Soft and fleecy clouds,
The blue sky above,
A baby's tiny hands,
The *coos* of morning doves,

The fragrance after rain,
A rainbow arching high,
A robin's cheery songs,
And an eagle in the sky.

Each day is a new beginning
Of the glories we have to share;
All are tokens of God's love,
For He has put them there.

Mother's Garden

Linda Ward
Eureka, California

I remember Mother's garden
And the flowers I loved best,
And, though all were very pretty,
The begonias led the rest.
The petunias were a riot,
Striped in pink and red and white;
The carnations smelled so lovely,
But their colors were not as bright.
The lilacs grew on bushes
That stood against the wall;
The pale pink rhododendron
Took forever to get tall.
In the planter near the stairway,
In a shady little spot
Where the ferns grew in abundance
And it never got too hot,
The begonias bloomed like jewels
In a pirate's treasure chest,
With deep hues of orange and yellow
And the red that I love best.
I remember Mother's garden
And the lesson that she taught:
If you have a love of flowers,
You've a wealth that can't be bought.

Mother's Green Thumb

Faye Adams
De Soto, Missouri

She has magic hands, the touch of Persephone. Everything she plants thrives vigorously. I recall the time she unwittingly produced blossoms from dead limbs. She stuck twigs, broken off a nearby tree, in dirt to mark the spots where she had planted seeds. When spring came, peach trees sprang up like Johnny-jump-ups, eager to do my mother's bidding.

"I don't need those any more," she said, as she pulled the markers out of the ground. But the sticks had taken root. And they soon became trees, thriving in my yard, blooming white in summer.

Readers are invited to submit original poetry for possible publication in future issues of IDEALS. *Please send typed copies only; manuscripts will not be returned. Writers receive payment for each published submission. Send material to Readers' Reflections, Ideals Publications, 535 Metroplex Drive, Suite 250, Nashville, Tennessee 37211.*

Quarter Notes

Helen C. Smith

Swallows on the telephone wires
Are quarter notes the sun inspires,
A rondo for the wind to play
Through the fields of new-mown hay.

Quarter notes on a sunlit staff—
My soul is not big enough by half
To hold the songs I hear today
Over the fields of sun-sweet hay.

I try to sing this wild, sweet song;
Then notes dart off and it goes wrong.
Yet still I hear the tunes they play
Above the fields in sunny May.

Memories

Elfreda Graham

Right here where sunshine warms the old stone wall,
Where scarlet hollyhocks once grew so tall,
Is just the place to linger and recall
The prick of earth on tender feet; the lure
Of wooded hillsides reached by paths obscure
And rough; the bluebird with his overture
To dawn; the smell of buckwheat bloom, choice haunt
Of thrifty bees; the peach that used to flaunt
Its fragile blossoms in the spring and taunt
Us with the promise of its ripened fruit;
The woods made magic with the thrush's flute
Or with the scarlet tanager's salute.
From memories such as these a charm is born
To deck the thistle and to gild the thorn.

*A path through Spanish bluebells invites visitors to Winterthur
Garden in Delaware. Photograph by William H. Johnson.*

*Overleaf: Dahlias bring the delight of sunshine and vivid
color to this cottage garden. Photograph by Toni
Schneiders/H. Armstrong Roberts.*

Simple Beauty

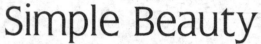
Shirley Sallay

A violet bloomed upon a hill,
Held tightly to its side;
The rocky crevice where it grew
Was worn by time and tide.

A seashell lay upon the shore,
Cast there by a foamy wave,
Reminder of the capacious deep,
A cool and dark blue cave.

An acorn fell beneath the oak
Upon a bed of leaves,
Unnoticed by the passing throng
On many days and eves.

A baby is born and man looks up
In thanks each day to God
For the gift of simple things on earth:
A blossom, shell, or pod.

*Cow parsnip flowers beside a waterfall on Grant Creek below Spray
Park in Mount Rainier National Park, Washington. Photograph by
Mary Liz Austin/Donnelly Austin Photography.*

Morning Song

Edith Nesbit

Baby darling, wake and see,
    Morning's here, my little rose;
Open eyes and smile at me
    Ere I clasp and kiss you close.
      Baby darling, smile, for then
      Mother sees the sun again.

Baby darling, sleep no more.
    All the other flowers have done
With their sleeping—you, my flower,
    Are the only sleepy one;
      All the pink-filled daisies shout:
      "Bring our little sister out!"

Baby darling, in the sun
    Birds are singing, sweet and shrill;
And my bird's the only one
    That is nested softly still.
      Baby, if you only knew,
      All the birds are calling you.

Baby darling, all is bright,
    God has brought the sunshine here;
And the sleepy silent night
    Comes back soon enough, my dear.
      Wake, my darling, night is done,
      Sunbeams call my little one.

*A kitten snoozes in a "just-right" flowerpot, oblivious to the beauty of
the surrounding flowers. Photograph by Nancy Matthews.*

SLICE OF LIFE

Edna Jaques

TO YOUNG MOTHERS

Take time to hear their prayers at night,
    And cuddle them a little bit;
Tell them a story now and then,
    And steal a little time to sit
And listen to their childish talk,
    Or take them for a little walk.

You do not know it now—but soon
    They will be gone (the years are swift),
For life just marches on and on,
    And heaven holds no sweeter gift
Than a small boy with tousled hair,
    Who leaves his toys just anywhere.

A picnic can be such a treat,
    With sand to play in clean and white,
When blue waves breaking on the shore
    Are filled with wonder and delight
For children armed with tins and pails
    And wooden boats with crooked sails.

Take time to laugh and sing and play,
    To really cherish and enjoy
A little girl with flaxen curls,
    And the small wonder of a boy;
They ask so little when they are small,
    Just love and tenderness—that is all.

*In this painting, entitled GOOD MEMORIES, artist Robert Duncan
captures the special quality of a shared moment.*

Are You Your Children's Confidant?

Laura Ingalls Wilder

—————————————— *1921* ——————————————

A letter from my mother, who is seventy-six years old, lies on my desk beside a letter from my daughter far away in Europe. Reading the message from my mother, I am a child again and a longing unutterable fills my heart for Mother's counsel, for the safe haven of her protection and the relief from responsibility which trusting in her judgment always gave me. But when I turn to the letter written by my daughter, who will always be a little girl to me no matter how old she grows, then I understand and appreciate my mother's position and her feelings toward me.

Many of us have the blessed privilege of being at the same time mother and child, able to let the one interpret the other to us until our understanding of both is full and rich. What is

> *The most universal sentiment in the world is that of mother-love.*

there in the attitude of your children toward yourself that you wish were different? Search your heart and learn if your ways toward your own mother could be improved.

In the light of experience and the test of years, can you see how your mother might have been more to you, could have guided you better?

Then be sure you are making the most of your privileges with the children who are looking to you for love and guidance. For there is, after all, no great difference between the generations; the problems of today and tomorrow must be met in much the same way as those of yesterday.

During the years since my mother was a girl to the time when my daughter was a woman, there have been many slight, external changes in the fashions and ways of living, some change in the thought of the world, and much more freedom in expressing those thoughts. But the love of mother and child is the same, with the responsibility of controlling and guiding on the one side and the obligation of obedience and respect on the other. The most universal sentiment in the world is that of mother-love. . . .In all ages, in all countries it is the same—a boundless, all-enveloping love; if necessary, a sacrifice of self for the offspring.

Think of the number of children in the world, each the joy of some mother's heart, each a link connecting one generation with another, each a hope for the future. It stuns the mind to contemplate their number and their possibilities, for these are the coming rulers of the world: the makers of destiny, not only for their own generation but for the generations to come. And they are being trained for their part in the procession of time by the women of today.

Special thoughts about those we love are reflected in our efforts to keep in touch. Photograph by Nancy Matthews.

FOR THE CHILDREN

A Gift for My Mother

Eileen Spinelli

There are lots of things
  that I could do for Mom
  on Mother's Day.
I could make her
  Sunday breakfast,
  set pink flowers
  on the tray.
I could use my week's
  allowance
  to buy chocolates
  in a box,
  or a jar of scented hand cream,
  or a pair of purple socks.
Any one of those
  would certainly
  delight a lot of mothers.
But the gift
  my mom wants most
  is this:
"Be nicer to your sister."

So I have made a promise
  to myself—
  to share my books and toys.
And not to yell, "Be quiet!"
  when my sister
  makes some noise.
I will be sure she wears
  her boots
  and takes an umbrella
  in the rain.
When she asks for help
  with schoolwork
I will give it—
  not complain.
Mom will wonder,
  ask: "What has happened
  to make you behave this way?"
I will grin, and then
I will hug her and say:
"Happy Mother's Day!"

SOMEONE TO REMEMBER

Marjorie L. Lloyd

MY MOTHER AND BOOKS

The earliest memory I have of my mother is the sound of her voice reading from a book as we perched on my bed as the afternoon sunlight warmed the room. With these words she once again brought me into the world of the imagination: "This the forest primeval./ The murmuring pines and the hemlocks." Her long brown hair framed her face as she quoted Longfellow's narrative poem, her voice rising and lowering with each turn in the story. Her dark blue eyes would keep glancing at me as if we were sharing something special, and she wanted me to enjoy it as much as she did.

My mother made the preliminary daily-nap ritual so exciting with the possibilities of the imagination that I was actually eager for naptime. As I slowly began to understand that clusters of letters stood for particular sounds, she allowed me to choose a book; and we would alternate reading paragraphs or verses, often taking weeks to finish one book. Before I officially started school, I was sruggling with *Hetty's First Hundred Years* and wanting more.

Her belief in the importance of sharing the written word was not limited to family. One of our neighbors was responsible for starting a small lending library in our church, and she asked my mother to take on the job of maintaining the library. Immediately Mother contacted the national church convention about the criteria for establishing a certified library. More than twenty years later the library had expanded to a large area next to the entrance of the church and had achieved several progressively more in-depth standards for church libraries. Mother became a consultant to librarians from other small churches, and it would not be exaggerating to state that her influence was felt by thousands of readers. Her motivation was always, "Let me share this book with you."

Mother often said that children were her best readers; she carefully purchased illustrated books that would appeal to children. My fondness for Eric Carle's books originated when I watched my

---

Coming home from school, I would often find my mother sitting at the dining table, surrounded by stacks of books.

---

mother sitting on the floor reading *Brown Bear, Brown Bear, What Do You See?* to a group of toddlers from a Sunday school class.

When the first Japanese family arrived in our community to help plan an automobile plant, they began to attend our church; and their young daughter was a frequent visitor to the library. She did not speak English but she loved picture books, particularly one about the Eskimos in Alaska. Soon Mother set out on a buying trip to purchase more children's books; she wanted this young girl to have books with children that "looked more like her."

Mother's commitment to sharing books was not superficial or just convenient, for she often spent much of her own household funds to acquire books, never expecting to be reimbursed by the church. As she stood in front of a display in the bookstore, she would murmur to herself, "Yvonne would like this," or "This would make a beautiful memorial book."

My mother included me in the book-buying process too. "Would you read this one?" she would ask as she thrust a Maurice Sendak book toward me. And so we would explore the bookstore together.

Spending a quiet moment to remember our loved ones is important in each of our lives.
Photograph by Nancy Matthews.

Coming home from school during my teen years, I often found my mother seated at the dining table, surrounded by stacks of books. She would catalog them and then complete extensive paperwork so that they would all be ready for next Sunday's use. As she worked, she would share some of her comments: "Eugenia Price

I still practice my mother's first and most memorable lesson.

knows Southern people," she would exclaim and then proceed to read a page or two of the author's newest novel, just as if I were still small enough to snuggle by her side.

Mother also began to write a weekly column for the Sunday bulletin, in which she would review new titles in the library and remind members of seasonal materials. Her humor, intelligence, and quiet strength are apparent in each line.

After my father died, my mother began to promote words in a slightly different way. After years of reading and sharing books, my mother began to write, and her articles about our hometown were published in a regional magazine.

I still practice my mother's first and most memorable lesson: reading every day. Today I hold a book in my hands with a sense of awe because my mother showed me new worlds and fascinating people within the pages of a book.

I comfortably share my mother's name; and I am thankful, when I look at my daughter and my son, who both read every day, that I learned the value of loving books from this remarkable woman.

Songs for My Mother:
Her Words

Anna Hempstead Branch

My mother has the prettiest tricks
   Of words and words and words.
Her talk comes out as smooth and sleek
   As breasts of singing birds.

She shapes her speech all silver fine
   Because she loves it so.
And her own eyes begin to shine
   To hear her stories grow.

And if she goes to make a call
   Or out to take a walk,
We leave our work when she returns
   And run to hear her talk.

We had not dreamed these things were so
   Of sorrow and of mirth.
Her speech is as a thousand eyes
   Through which we see the earth.

God wove a web of loveliness,
   Of clouds and stars and birds,
But made not any thing at all
   So beautiful as words.

They shine around our simple earth
   With golden shadowings,
And every common thing they touch
   Is exquisite with wings.

There's nothing poor and nothing small
   But is made fair with them.
They are the hands of living faith
   That touch the garment's hem.

They are as fair as bloom or air;
   They shine like any star;
And I am rich who learned from her
   How beautiful they are.

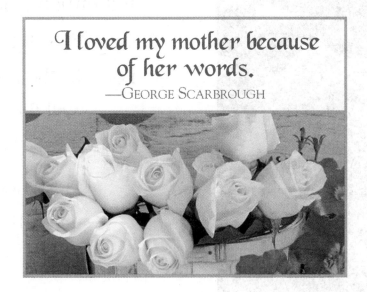

I loved my mother because of her words.
— GEORGE SCARBROUGH

Roses, whether growing in a garden or gathered into a bouquet, bring cheer to everyone. Photograph by Nancy Matthews.

My Mother's Voice

Laura Hope Marshall

I stand and wait
To hear a sound so sweet across the miles
That stills my racing heart,
And I am left serene and calm,
So reassured of love and satisfied.
No other sound can ever mean the same;
For when I am old and sands of time are low,
It will reverberate within my heart,
And I will know
There is no greater joy or sweeter melody
When my mother's voice rings clear and answers me.

Talk not of wasted affection,
            affection never was wasted,
If it enrich not the heart of another,
            its waters returning
Back to their springs, like the rain
            shall fill them full of refreshment;
That which the fountain sends forth
            returns again to the fountain.

—HENRY WADSWORTH LONGFELLOW

*In a forest near North Hilo, Hawaii, a waterfall flows among
beautiful wild flowers. Photograph by Christopher Talbot Frank.*

DEVOTIONS FROM THE HEART

Pamela Kennedy

Fix these words of mine in your hearts and minds. . . . Teach them to your children, talking about them when you sit at home and when you walk along the road, when you lie down and when you get up.
— *Deuteronomy 11:18-19* (NIV)

ALWAYS TEACHING

Recently, I was asked to speak to a group of young mothers about the importance of reading to children. I did quite a bit of research and enlisted the help of the excellent elementary librarian at the school where I teach. I wanted the latest thinking on learning and the brain, and she gave me some fascinating articles to read about current scientific studies and PET scans. As we talked, however, our conversation came around to what worked best with our own children. Even without the latest brain research, as mothers we knew that reading together with our children was about a lot more than enhanced neurons. But I wondered if our intuitions were true for others, so I decided to do an experiment of my own.

I teach sophomores at a college prep school for girls. One day, for their journal entry, I asked them to each write about a favorite story or book from their childhood. I expected to get a good list of storybooks to share with the young moms and perhaps a cute anecdote or two as well. What I received from my high school students turned out to be far more than that.

Almost without exception, the girls wrote not only about the books and stories they had loved, but also about the whole experience of being read to. Many students recalled being held in the circle of their mothers' arms, of laughing together, of seeing the smiles of approval on their mothers' faces when they read their first words.

Dear Father, I thank you for the opportunity to teach children about your faithfulness. May my lessons always be filled with truth and encouragement.

They wrote of feeling secure and loved and of knowing that, no matter what was going on in the world around them, this was a safe place to be. One student said that storytime was the only time when she and her brother could lie still, side by side, and not argue. Another said that when the character in her favorite story, a mischievous bunny, was loved despite all his flaws, she knew that her mother was saying the same thing to her.

My students' anecdotes were rich with the

lessons they had learned snuggled beside their mothers, yet the stories contained a wistful quality as well. These young women, who were struggling with adolescence and algebra, longed for those childhood feelings of safety once more. Despite chafing at the bit of parental authority, they still felt drawn to that place near their mothers' hearts where they had first learned about love and acceptance, wonder and truth.

Thousands of years ago, God spoke through Moses about the importance of parents teaching children. In the verses on the opposite page, it is clear that learning occurs in a variety of places and experiences. Teaching never ceases; we teach when we walk and talk, when we engage in recreation, and even when we rest. The oportunity for lessons are everywhere, but unless parents and grandparents teach them, they will go unlearned. Who

An 1850 cherry secretary and a child-size trestle table make pleasant reading places in this small country library. Photograph by Jessie Walker.

will tell our children about the legacy of faith, the stories of courage as well as of failure? Who will share the tales of family joy and sorrow, and the Lord's presence in them all?

When I finally spoke to the young mothers about the importance of reading to their youngsters, I began by sharing some of the stories my students had written. "Here is the real reason you want to read to your children," I said. "Reading is about more than language skills and intellect or brain studies and achievement. It is about building relationships that span generations. You mothers are the first teachers your children will have." As a mother, I relish the fact that we will always be teachers.

Pamela Kennedy is a freelance writer of short stories, articles, essays, and children's books. Wife of a retired naval officer and mother of three children, she has made her home on both U.S. coasts and currently resides in Honolulu, Hawaii.

Mother's Hands

W. Dayton Wedgefarth

Dear, gentle hands have stroked my hair
   And cooled my brow,
Soft hands that pressed me close and seemed
   To know somehow
Those fleeting moods and erring thoughts
   That cloud my day,
Which quickly melt beneath their suffrage
   And pass away.

No other balm for earthly pain
   Is half so sure,
No sweet caress so filled with love
   Nor half so pure,
No other soul so close akin
   That understands,
No touch that brings such perfect peace
   As Mother's hands.

Beautiful Hands

Jessie Cannon Eldridge

Beautiful hands are the hands that do
The tasks that the Lord gave them to,
The homely tasks that, day by day,
Make life easier along the way
For other people; that wash and cook
And make of a house a comfortable nook
That folks like to come to; that scrub and scour;
That soothe and heal no matter the hour.
Floors, clothes, and dishes, across our lands,
Are made clean again by beautiful hands.

*In a sunlit solarium, an inviting table is set for brunch as
a special occasion. Photograph by Jessie Walker.*

THROUGH MY WINDOW

Pamela Kennedy

STITCHES IN TIME

Needlework goes way back in my family tree. My Grandma had a framed commendation from the Red Cross for having knitted dozens of pairs of wool socks for soldiers during World Wars I and II. Grandma learned to knit in England. I remember her telling me that the girls in her school had to make their own long winter stockings. At the time she told me this, I was in elementary school, and I could not imagine anything more torturous. I pictured my chubby grandmother as a small, pale child sitting next to Oliver Twist, eating gruel and knitting stockings. My imaginings were probably far more colorful than the actual facts, but they sure put me off knitting.

My associations with sewing, however, were more positive. My mother belonged to only one club. She said it was because there was "too much gossip and too little good" going on in most of them. But the Sewing Club was different. Back in the early 1950s, on Wednesday nights, several of the neighbor women gathered to share patterns and material scraps. While there may have been a little gossiping, there was a lot more good going on. Maybe I thought this because every Christmas I received the most wonderful bounty of handmade doll clothes a young girl could imagine. There were a bride's dress complete with seed pearls and crystal beads, formal gowns made of real silk brocade, woolen coats with mink collars, print daytime dresses and pedal pushers, and even an elegant organza nightgown and negligee trimmed with tiny satin roses and ribbons.

As time passed, the Sewing Club members drifted apart; but my mother's talents were not put on the shelf. She made blouses and skirts for school and a new dress for every high-school

---

Back in the early 1950s, on Wednesday nights, several of the neighbor women gathered to share patterns and material scraps.

---

prom. We would go to Murray's Fine Fabrics a month or so before the dance, choose a pattern and fabric, and then I'd watch in amazement as my mother turned yards of satin or velveteen or chiffon into beautiful dresses and gowns.

I was determined to learn to sew; but, as often happens between mothers and daughters, my lessons were not very productive. She was too proficient and I was too impatient. In a demonstration of great wisdom, she suggested I sign up for home economics and learn to sew at school. My first project was a butcher apron made from beige cotton. It wasn't very exciting, but I did learn to sew along a curve and turn a hem. After that I went on to more advanced classes where we made dresses with collars, facings, darts, gathers, set-in sleeves, buttonholes, zippers, the works. By the end of the class, I thought I was ready for anything. Then I went off to college and sewing seemed a waste of time.

After I married my young Navy officer, however, I realized that my sewing machine was going to be a lifesaver. On a tiny budget, living in cramped apartments and military quarters, I could change a cheap cotton remnant into a pair of curtains and give our place a whole new look. I created placemats, tablecloths, shower curtains, and draperies over the years, often turning one into another as we moved and window sizes changed. And then the children came along. There was no need for me to buy expensive rompers or dresses. After three weeks at a class, I was whipping up shirts for everyone too.

But the biggest challenge came when the kids entered school. I never realized how many costumes it takes to help a child successfully graduate from an institution of education. Of course, there were Halloween costumes, but there were patterns for those. I created bunny suits, superhero togs, Indian outfits, and even a black panther costume complete with a stuffed tail and satin-lined ears! No, the real challenges came from creative history and literature teachers and my children's penchant for pushing deadlines.

"Hey, Mom, did I tell you I have to go to school dressed as a storybook character—tomorrow?" I would hear. Or "Mom, do you have anything that can make me look like a signer of the Declaration of Independence? I need it in twenty minutes."

My creative juices would kick in. An old black cape from a vampire costume and a quickly re-designed Pilgrim's hat became evening wear for Thomas Jefferson as he rushed to history class just in time to put his name on the dotted line! The Halloween Indian suit transformed into Rumpelstiltskin when I whacked off the fringe, created a beard from quilt batting, and sewed a square of fabric into a cone for a hat. *Voila!* My son was ready for English class in under half an hour!

It was a long way from Grandma's stockings, but the stitches in those projects had just as much love. Sewing allowed me to connect with my family, passing along gifts of hand and heart. My daughter, who had just graduated from college and was always too busy for domestic chores, confided to me a few months ago that she thinks she needs to learn to sew. I smiled, for I have a feeling she will soon be making her own stitches in time!

Original art by Doris Ettlinger.

Painting in Thread

John Evan Carson

Crossing the stitch,
Painting in thread,
Using a lap
For an easel instead—
Colors strung through
A needled brush,
Weaving the hues
So deep and so lush.

Pictures that take
So much time,
Stitched with love
Into patterns that rhyme.
The patient artist,
Her skillful touch
Creating the works
That mean so much.

Pillows and blankets,
Quilts and bibs,
Covers for tables
And baby cribs—
Heirlooms that warm,
Comfort, and hold;
Each one worth
Its weight in gold.

Some artists paint
Or work in clay;
Some sell their work
Or give it away.
Others hand it down
     instead—
Crossing the stitch
And painting in thread.

Cradle Quilt

June Masters Bacher

The quilt that cradled as sweetly you slept—
Did you trace its pattern of memories kept?
Captured in abstract,
Circle and square,
To cross-stitch distance
From here to there:
A block of black velvet
From Granny's chair,
A first-day-of-school skirt,
Locks of your hair,
An ivory petticoat's clinging caress,
A taffeta whisper of wedding dress—
Cloth-binding of a patchwork of shapeless things
Created from chaos and given wings.

*A warm cup of tea provides a relaxing moment. Photograph by
Dianne Dietrich Leis/Dietrich Leis Stock Photography.*

A Mother's Love

Thomas Burbidge

A little in the doorway sitting,
The mother plied her busy knitting,
And her cheek so softly smil'd,
You might be sure, although her gaze
Was on the meshes of the lace,
Yet her thoughts were with her child.
But when the boy had heard her voice,
As o'er her work she did rejoice,
His became silent altogether,
And slyly creeping by the wall,
He seiz'd a single plume, let fall
By some wild bird of longest feather;
And all a-tremble with his freak,
He touch'd her lightly on the cheek.

Oh, what a loveliness her eyes
Gather in that one moment's space,
While peeping round the post she spies
Her darling's laughing face!
Oh, mother's love is glorifying,
On the cheek like sunset lying;
In the eyes a moisten'd light,
Softer than the moon at night!

*A young girl shares her secrets of the sea with her
mother in this painting entitled* Listening to the
Sea, *by Mary Louise Gow (1851-1929). Image
from Fine Art Photographic Library, Ltd., London.*

Good Thoughts

Katherine Maurine Haaff

Good thoughts are the threads
With which we weave the web of life,
The threads which build
The strong and fibrous cloth
We know as character.
And, like the patterns
That looms of modern science weave,
Our lives can be no lovelier,
No stronger, than the threads
From which our lives are made.

My Mother's Shawl

George L. Kress

I remember winter nights
When I was put to bed,
After Mother dimmed the lights
And all my prayers were said.

I remember how she tucked
The quilted covers round
And the way, deep-down, I ducked,
Like going underground.

I remember how the gale
Kept pounding on the roof
Like an angry dragon's tail
Or else a dragon's hoof.

I remember how the sound
Kept fading far away.

With a start, I woke and found,
Amazingly, it was day!

Then I saw my bedstead wore
A spread that covered all;
Something red, not there before—
My mother's knitted shawl.

So she had tiptoed as I slept
To lay its warming fold,
So my body snug was kept
Against the growing cold.

Now as I grow old,
When cruel fates befall,
In the dawn, against the cold,
I find her spreading shawl.

Vintage towels and tablecloths are stacked beneath hats,
perfect for long walks outside. Photograph by Jessie Walker.

FROM AMERICA'S ATTIC

Lois Winston

SEWING MACHINE

As a very young child, I used to take my dolls for seesaw rides, not on the playground but on a movable metal grate attached to a cabinet in the second floor hallway of my grandmother's home. Years later, I learned that my makeshift seesaw was my great-grandmother's Singer treadle sewing machine.

Like many families in the late 1800s, mine probably bought their machine from

I never forgot the fun of crawling under that cabinet and taking my dolls for a ride.

Singer by paying five dollars down, half an average weekly salary in those days, and three to five dollars a month thereafter until the principal and interest were paid off. This special purchase was notable for many families because the sewing machine was actually the first machine to become a part of the American home. It was seen as somewhat of a miracle when first introduced.

Although most school textbooks credit Elias Howe, Jr. with the invention, many individuals, going back to Thomas Saint in 1790, contributed to its development. In 1850, Isaac Merrit Singer developed the first practical sewing machine and thereby began a legend. Singer made a significant design change. Whereas previous machines had employed a hand crank to power the needle, Singer developed a treadle mechanism to replace the hand crank.

An 1860 issue of *Scientific American* called the sewing machine the most important invention to the world, bested by only the spinning Jenny and the plow. *Godey's Lady's Book*, a popular women's magazine, dubbed the sewing machine "The Queen of Inventions." These praises were written because the time needed to make an average shirt, for example, was reduced from ten to fourteen hours down to a little more than an hour when a machine was used.

Singer's company soon became the world's largest manufacturer of mass-produced sewing machines. Singer was eventually awarded twenty-one patents. By 1876, his company was selling twice as many sewing machines as his closest competitor. By 1890, Singer's company had produced nine million sewing machines.

The machines were expensive, however, for the average American; and even with pay-

In 1850, Isaac Merrit Singer developed the first practical sewing machine and began a legend.

ment plans, the price was out of reach for many households. My great-grandmother must have considered her purchase important enough to set up an installment plan. In some communities, organizations often pooled their money to purchase a single machine for communal use. But as sewing machine production and sales increased, the price soon dropped. More families were able to afford a sewing machine of their own; and, by 1910, a sewing machine could be found in most homes.

Several significant innovations accompanied the sewing machine's growing sales and accessibility. In 1873, Helen Augusta Blanchard of Portland, Maine, invented the still popular zig-zag stitch; and, by 1905, machines could be run on electric power. Today more than four thousand different types of sewing machines are manufactured, including those with amazing features such as computerized embroidery—something my great-grandmother could never have conceived.

Purchasing a sewing machine today can be a complicated decision. And none of the new ones have the graceful curves, gold decorations, and elaborate cabinets that were common to the old ones.

I have no idea what happened to my great-grandmother's treadle machine. During my teen years, my grandmother sold her house and moved into an apartment; the treadle did not make the move with her. But I never forgot the fun of crawling under that cabinet and taking my dolls for a ride.

Years ago, I happened upon a yard sale, and there on the lawn stood a standard treadle machine. "How much?" I asked the owner.

A nineteenth-century woman is depicted in this illustration for an advertising campaign for the Singer sewing machine. Image courtesy of Singer Sewing Company. Copyright © Singer Sewing Company. All rights reserved.

"You can have it for fifteen dollars," he replied. Although I prefer to sew on my ultra-modern machine, for over thirty years that old treadle machine has occupied a place of honor in my home.

Lois Winston is a freelance writer and designer whose work appears regularly in craft and women's magazines. Her home is in New Jersey.

BITS & PIECES

Most of all the other beautiful things in life come by twos and threes, by dozens and hundreds. Plenty of roses, stars, sunsets, rainbows, brothers and sisters, aunts and cousins, but only one mother in the whole world.

—*Kate Douglas Wiggin*

In one a trio, beautiful,
Grandmother, loving daughter,
    loving daughter's daughter, sat,
Chatting and sewing.

—*Walt Whitman*

She looketh well to
the ways of her household.

—*Proverbs 31:27*

Thou are thy mother's glass, and she in thee
Calls back the lovely April of her prime.

—*William Shakespeare*

A mother is the best friend anyone ever has.
—*Author Unknown*

*T*here never was a great man
who had not a great mother.
—*Olive Schrienier*

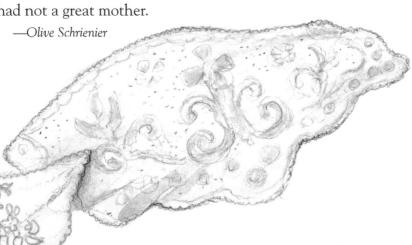

*O*f all the flavors one eats, salt is indispensable; wherever
one goes in the world, one's mother is dearest.
—*Chinese Proverb*

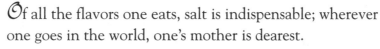

I can remember no time when I did not understand that
my mother must write books because people would have
and read them; but I cannot remember one hour in
which her children needed her and did not find her.
—*Elizabeth Stuart Phelps*

*F*or if my father was the head of our house,
my mother was its heart.
—*Philip Dunne*

I would weave you a song, my mother.
—*Madeleine Mason-Manheim*

*S*he who knows how to do fine sewing can
make things beautiful enough for anyone.
—*Emily Post*

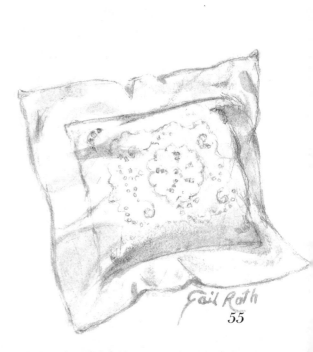

Gail Roth
55

Mother's Aprons
Harriet Whipple

I recall the kind of aprons
That Mother used to wear;
She seldom was without one,
All starched and ironed with care.
While her apron saved her dresses,
It had other uses too—
Like bringing in some ripened plums
Or vegetables she grew.
Her apron made a handy fan
When days were very warm,
And it brought in all the laundry
When hit by sudden storm.
It also covered up her arms
When she stepped out in the cold,
And it carried all the mended socks
That she had neatly rolled.
Her apron made a handy basket
For eggs she gathered too
Or her fresh-cut climbing roses,
Still wet with morning dew.
The apron hung behind the door
When she had gone away,
And I still see her in that apron
Within my heart today.

Her Checkered Apron
Linnea Bodman

Stored in a trunk in the attic,
    Forgotten for many a year,
I found Mother's big checkered apron,
    So familiar to me and so dear.

I still see her sitting and peeling
    The peaches and pears that she canned,
Then screwing the lids on the glass jars
    With a corner of it in her hand.

Made from a square of checked cotton,
    Practical, simple, and plain,
It was handy on many occasions
    And served her again and again—

Not only while cooking and cleaning,
    But also for carrying things
Such as apples or kindling or kittens,
    Or flowers that summertime brings,

Or gathering eggs from the henhouse,
    Shooing away a mad bee,
Flicking the crumbs from the table,
    Or shining an apple for me.

And two of its comforting functions
    Were drying a crying child's eyes
And wrapping him up in its vastness
    While she cuddled away his hurt sighs.

Now back it will go where I found it,
    Its edges all neatly aligned.
But the memories stored in its sweet folds
    Will endure for all time in my mind.

Teapots, pottery, pink Depression glassware, and pillows made from vintage linens, make a pastel collage for a comfortable retreat. Photograph by Jessie Walker.

The Damask Tablecloth

Nellie Varnes Fultz

Each special day at our house
Was always sure to bring
Out Mother's pansy pattern
As a festive covering;
Full twelve feet long, it glistened,
All grand and snowy-white,
With pansies here and pansies there
To Mother's great delight.

I often think how Mother
Did not have so very much
Of worldly goods like we have now,
Lace tablecloths and such;
But what she had she cherished;
And, she did not ask for wealth,
But got her joy from other things
Like love and home and health.

Mother's pansy pattern
Was always put away
Well-wrapped in blue paper
In the top of the buffet;
It didn't share the quarters
Of the common things, oh no,
But was most especially sheltered
Like a rare old cameo.

Mother's pansy pattern,
On countless glad birthdays,
Now seems to me a symbol
Of Mother's gentle ways,
Of the joy of family living
And Mother's faith in life—
That God would watch her children
And see them safe through strife.

FAMILY RECIPES

The wonderful aromas from the kitchens of our mothers and grandmothers are memories we all treasure. Share these favorite cakes from our readers with your own family and create some new memories. We would love to read your favorite recipe too. Send a typed copy to Ideals Publications, 535 Metroplex Drive, Suite 250, Nashville, Tennessee 37211. Payment will be provided for each recipe published.

Strawberry Jam Cake

Agnes G. White, Hoffman, Illinois

2	cups flour	2	eggs
½	teaspoon nutmeg	¾	cup buttermilk
1	teaspoon cinnamon	1	cup strawberry jam
1	teaspoon baking soda	½	cup pecans, chopped
1	cup butter	1	cup confectioners' sugar
1	cup granulated sugar		

Preheat oven to 350°F. In a medium bowl, sift together flour, nutmeg, cinnamon, and baking soda. Set aside. In a large bowl, cream butter and granulated sugar. Add eggs and buttermilk; mix well. Stir dry ingredients into butter mixture, mixing well. Stir in jam and pecans. Pour into a greased 8- x 12-inch baking pan. Bake 45 minutes or until toothpick inserted into middle comes out clean. Sprinkle warm cake with confectioners' sugar. Makes 16 servings.

Easy Lemon Pound Cake

Chris Bryant, Johnson City, Tennessee

1	8-ounce package cream cheese	½	cup milk
4	eggs	1	tablespoon grated lemon zest
1	package yellow cake mix		

Preheat oven to 350°F. In a large bowl, whip cream cheese until light and fluffy. Add eggs, one at a time, beating well. Stir in cake mix alternately with milk, beating just until combined. Stir in lemon zest. Pour mixture into a greased tube pan. Bake 55 minutes or until toothpick inserted in cake comes out clean. Makes 16 servings.

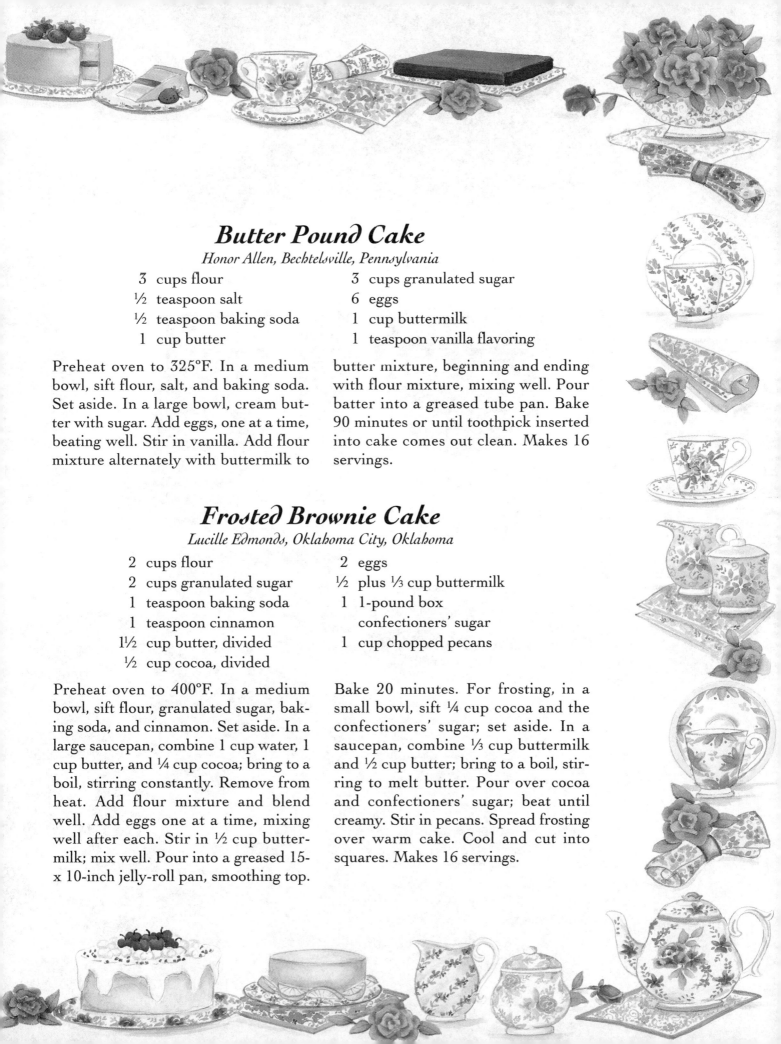

Butter Pound Cake

Honor Allen, Bechtelsville, Pennsylvania

3 cups flour	3 cups granulated sugar
½ teaspoon salt	6 eggs
½ teaspoon baking soda	1 cup buttermilk
1 cup butter	1 teaspoon vanilla flavoring

Preheat oven to 325°F. In a medium bowl, sift flour, salt, and baking soda. Set aside. In a large bowl, cream butter with sugar. Add eggs, one at a time, beating well. Stir in vanilla. Add flour mixture alternately with buttermilk to butter mixture, beginning and ending with flour mixture, mixing well. Pour batter into a greased tube pan. Bake 90 minutes or until toothpick inserted into cake comes out clean. Makes 16 servings.

Frosted Brownie Cake

Lucille Edmonds, Oklahoma City, Oklahoma

2 cups flour	2 eggs
2 cups granulated sugar	½ plus ⅓ cup buttermilk
1 teaspoon baking soda	1 1-pound box confectioners' sugar
1 teaspoon cinnamon	1 cup chopped pecans
1½ cup butter, divided	
½ cup cocoa, divided	

Preheat oven to 400°F. In a medium bowl, sift flour, granulated sugar, baking soda, and cinnamon. Set aside. In a large saucepan, combine 1 cup water, 1 cup butter, and ¼ cup cocoa; bring to a boil, stirring constantly. Remove from heat. Add flour mixture and blend well. Add eggs one at a time, mixing well after each. Stir in ½ cup buttermilk; mix well. Pour into a greased 15- x 10-inch jelly-roll pan, smoothing top. Bake 20 minutes. For frosting, in a small bowl, sift ¼ cup cocoa and the confectioners' sugar; set aside. In a saucepan, combine ⅓ cup buttermilk and ½ cup butter; bring to a boil, stirring to melt butter. Pour over cocoa and confectioners' sugar; beat until creamy. Stir in pecans. Spread frosting over warm cake. Cool and cut into squares. Makes 16 servings.

Old Houses
Homer D'Lettuso

There is comfort in old houses,
    Like a mother's arm or a friend's kind words.
There is joy in time-scarred timbers,
    In slated roofs and weathered boards.
      I am one with an old house;
         I am one with its pains and joys;
      An old house shared the travail of my mother;
      An old house shared my baby toys.

Old houses have a blessed look
    That is one with God's great plan.
Old houses have a tenderness,
    From the baby's crawl to the stride of the man.
      I am one with an old house;
         I am one with its kind embrace;
      An old house shared my mother's love;
      An old house knew my mother's lovely face.

I Know a Place
June Masters Bacher

I know a place that character built,
A place where great sacrifice
Was made to bring joy to all others;
I called it my paradise.
I know a place where happiness dwelt,
Where true love took its abode
And offered wide arms of shelter
To feet grown weary of roads.
Square feet would not measure the distance
From front door to the back;
Its spirit lit eyes of the children—
Windows that brightened night's black.
A sign said, "Come in without knocking,
Strangers no longer need roam."
Its atmosphere whispered a welcome—
My memory of Grandmother's home.

*Bright red geraniums and other lush flowers accentuate
this path at Butchart Gardens in Brentwood Bay on
Vancouver Island, British Columbia. Photograph by
H. Abernathy/H. Armstrong Roberts.*

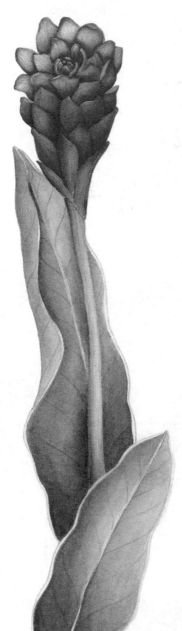

Faith
Author Unknown

"Keep this for me."
What child has not said this
And placed a treasure in his mother's hand
With strict injunction she should keep it safe
Till he return?
He knows with her it will be safe;
No troubled thought or anxious fear besets his mind,
And off he runs lighthearted to his play.
If children can so trust, why cannot we,
And place our treasures too in God's safe hand;
Our hopes, ambitions, needs, and those we love,
Just see them, in His all-embracing care,
And say with joyous heart, "They are with Thee."

A Mother's Prayer
Joyce Butler Miller

Lord, keep me faithful in little things,
Willingly doing the tasks each day brings.
Help me be loving and humble, I pray,
Tenderly showing to others Thy way.
And, dear Lord, when I long so to do
Some mighty work to show my deep love for You,
Then help me remember, oh, dear King of kings,
I must be faithful in little things.

When a Mother Prays
Grace V. Watkins

Sometimes when I have heard a mother pray
It seemed as though I heard a violin
Singing in silver loveliness the way
It sang across a twilight once within
A spring wood. And sometimes I have thought
That in a mother's prayer I heard the sound
Of brooks, lyric with playful wind, and caught
The low, unhurried music of the ground.
The glory in her voice is like the birth
Of music from the aisles of space, more fair
And beautiful than any song of earth.
And always, listening to a mother's prayer,
My heart is filled with wonder, knowing that she
Looks through a window on eternity.

Wildflowers bloom unexpectedly by a stream in Uncompahgre
National Forest in Colorado. Photograph by Christopher Talbot Frank.

A Mother's Creed

Sue Lennon

To be a credit to myself
And to the ones I love;
To realize that what I am
Is sent from God above;
To take the life that is given me
And make each moment count;
To keep my eyes and heart upon
The Sermon on the Mount;
To always see the beauty in
The freshly fallen snow;
To never cease to marvel at
How nature's wonders grow;
To make my faith the cornerstone
Of home and family life;
To help insure serenity,
Instead of stress and strife;
To know that God is the unseen hub
Around which we revolve;
That with His help no problem is
Too great for us to solve;
To face the future full of faith,
Though it be bright or dim—
The standard of our family life
Reflects our love of Him.

FROM MY MOTHER, [I LEARNED] PIETY
AND BENEFICENCE, AND ABSTINENCE,
NOT ONLY FROM EVIL DEEDS, BUT
EVEN FROM EVIL THOUGHTS, AND
FURTHER SIMPLICITY IN MY WAY OF
LIVING, FAR REMOVED FROM THE
HABITS OF THE RICH.

—MARCUS AURELIUS ANTONINUS

Purple clematis embraces a small birdhouse.
Photograph by Nancy Matthews.

Inset: The delicate beauty of a clematis is captured in this detail of a bloom in
Veldheer Gardens, Holland, Michigan. Photograph by Darryl R. Beers.

APPRECIATION

Pauline S. Walker

My mother was a poet; it was she
Who pointed out the beautiful to me:
Spirea branches gemmed by April rain;
The wind-waves on a sea of golden grain;
The lonely, lovely mists that rise and dip
At night like some great phantom treasure ship;
A stand of birch like altar candles white;
The moon's star-studded snood of twinkling light;
Frost-feathered elms against a wintry sky;
A wavering wedge of wild geese flying high.

My mother never penned a single part
Of any poem, yet wrote upon my heart
A love of beauty, and I will always be
So grateful for this precious legacy.

KNOWLEDGE

Author Unknown

We search the world for truth;
We cull the good, the pure, the beautiful
From graven stone and written scroll,
From the old flower-fields of the soul;
And weary seekers for the best,
We come back laden from our quest
To find that all the sages said
Is in the Book our mothers read.

Two variations of life's pleasures, roses and poetry, are depicted in this painting by Mary Kay Krell, entitled POETRY AND THE ROSE II. *Copyright © Mary Kay Krell. All rights reserved. Photograph by Steve Beasley.*

HOMETOWN AMERICA

D. Fran Morley

KNOX, INDIANA

When I was about five years old, I had the notion that small towns, such as the one I lived in, existed only in northern Indiana and that cities and towns everyplace else were bigger and more exciting. I have not a clue as to how I got this idea, but I do remember being surprised when, on a family car trip, I discovered that there were other small towns in other states.

In the late 1950s and early 1960s, about thirty-eight hundred people lived in Knox. The town was big enough to have a sense of identity but small enough to be a safe and secure place in which to live. I recall Knox as one of those fabled places where people did not bother to lock their doors and kids could play outside all day long without alarming their parents. It is not true, of course, that everyone knows everyone else in a small town, but it certainly seemed that way to me. I knew that if I got into trouble at one end of town, the news would quickly travel to my mother at the other end of town.

I clearly remember how my world expanded as I grew older. At first, I was limited to the sidewalk in front of my house, and later I was allowed to walk all the way around the block.

Finally, I received the sure sign of independence, permission to cross the street on my own! Many days I walked or rode my bike around town for hours on end, usually with friends, but sometimes on my own. On those solitary occasions, I whiled away the time making up stories in my head, imagining what was going on in every house I passed or with every person I saw on the street.

I loved walking downtown, or "uptown," as everyone called it then. During my childhood years, shops of every sort filled storefronts in the two-block section of Main Street in between the Nickel Plate Railroad on the south to the Starke County Courthouse on the north. Looking back, I remember an amazing array of businesses for such a small town; of course, most no longer

To my young eyes, it was the most magnificent structure that ever existed.

exist there today. Among the businesses, I recall a bakery, two dime stores, two groceries, a movie theater, two drug stores, two jewelry stores, a library, and several restaurants. The post office, with its marble floors and high windows, was always cool, even on the hottest summer afternoons. Across the street was a tiny shoe-repair shop; I can still smell the exotic odors that always hung in the air, a blend of leathers, machine oils, and shoe polishes.

As a little girl, the trips I took with my mother uptown were for business; she paid bills, ran errands, and bought groceries that we carried home in paper sacks. When I walked uptown with my dad on Saturdays, we headed for the sporting goods store, where I learned early lessons in biology by following the lifecycle of tadpoles kept in the big bait tank.

In all of uptown, my favorite building was the courthouse, and I am happy to say that it is preserved as an historic site

The Starke County Courthouse has been designated an historic site. Photograph by Patricia Atkinson.

today. The courthouse stands on a slight hill, making it look even more massive than it is. To my young eyes, it was the most magnificent structure that ever existed. Built of tan-colored limestone blocks, it has a red tile roof and a tall, four-sided clock tower that reaches high into the sky, making it visible from blocks away in any direction. The clock tower was always a homing beacon of sorts for me. It reassured me to know that if I climbed up into my tree house in my own backyard, I could see the tower above the trees of town.

By the time I reached high school, my fascination with my hometown had diminished considerably. Like others of my generation, I wanted nothing more than to move on to bigger cities and more exciting places. Now, I look back on my small town childhood with fond memories. I know that, contrary to my early belief, Knox is not so unique after all, but that is a good thing. I am thankful that I had the opportunity to grow up there at that particular place in time.

Fran Morley is a freelance writer and lives with her husband, Tom, and their cat, Gracie, in Fairhope, Alabama.

Daughter-in-Law
Vera E. Maddry

My daughter-in-law and I
Have such a lot of fun
Playing and planning work we know
Never will be done.

We have so much to talk about,
So many things to do;
We don't have time for worrying
Or feeling dull and blue.

I love the one that she adores;
She likes my "dearest" too;
We are both in love with a charming boy
Whose eyes are deepest blue.

Now where did I get her, you may ask,
Or where did she find me?
We met one day in a young man's heart
Quite by accident, you see.

A Son Marries
Nelle Hardgrove

Nothing is dearer to a mother's heart
Than a son, this is so true,
And through the years you often think
"When he is grown, what will I do?"
For then another woman
Will enter his life one day,
And all at once there are wedding bells
And she has stolen him away.
This is not bad, I have come to find;
I am now a mother-in-law
(That most maligned and dreaded state,
As history can avow).
Yet nothing has really changed for me,
And I am happy through and through,
For I find the love that once was his
Can stretch enough for two.

Something You Should Know
Author Unknown

Forgive me if I speak possessively of him
    Who now is yours, yet still is mine;
Call it the silver cord disparagingly
    And weave new colors in an old design,
Yet know the warp was started long ago
    By faltering steps, by syllable and sound,
By all the years in which I watched him grow,
    By all the seasons' turnings are we bound.
But now, I loose the cord, untie the knot,
    Unravel years so he is yours alone,
And if there is a message I forgot
    Or something that could help you had you known,
I shall be waiting, hoping you will see
    That him you love is also loved by me.

The Family Album

Cecil B. Smith

Pictures of the family,
Each one a memory brings
Of happy days and laughter,
Of tears, and many other things.
As I turn the pages
Of the album, one by one,
I recall so many times
That we all had so much fun.
Now, when days are more calm,
I find deep pleasure here—
With pictures of our family,
Getting larger every year.

Her Mother

Wilma Rose Westphal

Who listened well, as a dear friend's part,
To the secrets in a young girl's heart?
Who gave her counsel and urged her on
From childhood through to a bright new dawn?
Who helped that girl on her wedding day
While she smiled and dashed a tear away?
    Why, yes, it was her mother.

*Equipped with a basket perfect for carrying flowers,
a bicycle rests in a meadow blooming with wild lupine
in Los Padres National Forest, California.
Photograph by Londie G. Padelsky.*

She Is Loved

Maud Dawson

At her entrance into this world
I wept and then smiled—
How long we had waited
For this precious child.
Her laugh, her smile were our joy in life.
Toward each day she hurled
All her energy and eager hope.
And as the years went by,
I wept and then smiled
Because I knew there would come a day
When she would walk away
From us to another,
In love and eager to become
The woman that each day we
Knew we would see.
The day arrived in loveliness framed,
And I wept and then smiled,
For this is the mother's heart—
Receive, then give what you most love,
That beautiful, sweet, most precious child.

Mother
Roy Z. Kemp

She guided me through childhood's endless maze
With tender, loving hands, and guarded me
And sheltered me from life when it would daze,
And taught me how to pray with piety.

She knew my coming first and would have given
Her very life that I might breathe and live.
A mother's heart so willingly is surrendered
To charity and love. She will freely give.

I cannot repay her willing sacrifice;
I feel unworthy of so great a love;
On mothers' love, there is no earthly price—
It is a sacred thing from God above.

Dear Father, knowing all that she has done,
I pray, in love, make me a worthy son!

A Mother's Worth
Georgia B. Adams

Even if the whole world could be mine,
With every single wish at my command,
And if I had the widest choice of friends,
Sweetly fulfilled in my well-laid plans,
And if I were to choose
What in life mattered most to me,
I know, beyond a shadow of a doubt,
'Twould be my mother, yes, it would be she.
Who else through life, except my God above,
Remained steadfast, unmovable, and true?

Who, with a word of love and patient care,
Bore me up and every wave subdued?
Who gave unstintingly of herself
And never counted costs, though vast they were?
I only know that God loaned her to me,
And I will always love and cherish her.
Though the kings of this world have wealth untold
And their coffers overflow with jewels rare,
When one has a mother valued at great price
No earthly things can quite compare.

Vibrant hydrangea blossoms are perfectly framed by green foliage in a garden on Vashon Island, Washington. Photograph by Terry Donnelly/Donnelly Austin Photography.

Sculptor

Irene Taylor

Wonderful Mother,
Uncaring of fame,
Lovely memories return
At the sound of your name.
My glorious mentor,
You stilled fears
Through all of my
Youthful, wandering years.
Today, set aside,
Special honors are due;
Dearest one, in my heart,
Every day honors you.

Thanks

Joy Belle Burgess

How can I thank you, Mother,
For your tender, loving care,
For your warm, embracing arms,
And your softly whispered prayers?

How can I ever thank you
For your faith and guiding hand,
For your gentle, loving heart
That always understands?

How can I thank you, Mother,
For the courage you instill,
For words of hope that lead me on
To a grander dream fulfilled?

How can I ever thank you
For the blessings you impart,
For all the tenderness of love
That overflows your heart?

Petals from cherry trees decorate this brick garden path at Oak Hill in Mount Berry, Georgia. Photograph by William H. Johnson.

The Name of Mother

Fanny J. Crosby

The light, the spell-word of the heart,
    Our guiding star in weal or woe,
Our talisman, our earthly chart—
    That sweetest name that earth can know.

We breathed it first with lisping tongue
    Then cradled in her arms we lay;
Fond memories round that name are hung
    That will not, cannot pass away.

We breathed it then; we breathe it still,
    More dear than sister, friend or brother;
The gentle power, the magic thrill
    Awakened by the name of Mother.

Our Mother

Author Unknown

How often some passing word will tend
    In visions to recall
Our truest, dearest, fondest friend—
    That earliest friend of all

Who tended on our childish years,
    Those years that pass as hours,
When all earth's dewy, trembling tears
    Lie hidden within her flowers.

Thou star that shines in darkest night,
    When most we need thy aid,
Nor changes but to beam more bright
    When others coldly fade.

Hydrangeas, lilies, yellow coreopsis, and other lovely flowers surround this charming cottage. Photograph by Jessie Walker.

A Day
William L. Stidger

What does it take to make a day?
A lot of love along the way:
It takes a morning and a noon,
A father's voice, a mother's croon;
It takes some task to challenge all
The powers that a man may call
His own: the powers of mind and limb;
A whispered word of love; a hymn
Of hope—a comrade's cheer—
A baby's laughter and a tear;
It takes a dream, a hope, a cry
Of need from some soul passing by;
A sense of brotherhood and love;
A purpose sent from God above;
It takes a sunset in the sky,
The stars of night, the winds that sigh;
It takes a breath of scented air,
A mother's kiss, a baby's prayer.
That is what it takes to make a day:
A lot of love along the way.

*Inset: Freshly cut iris blooms rest on a garden sundial.
Photograph by Dick Dietrich/Dietrich Leis Stock Photography.*

*Irises bloom in a late-spring garden in Bristol, New
Hampshire. Photograph by William H. Johnson.*

Nature

Emily Dickinson

Nature, the gentlest mother,
Impatient of no child,
The feeblest or the waywardest—
Her admonition mild

In forest and the hill
By traveller is heard,
Restraining rampant squirrel
Or too impetuous bird.

How fair her conversation,
A summer afternoon—
Her household, her assembly;
And when the sun goes down

Her voice among the aisles
Incites the timid prayer
Of the minutest cricket,
The most unworthy flower.

When all the children sleep
She turns as long away
As will suffice to light her lamps;
Then bending from the sky,

With infinite affection
And infinite care,
Her golden finger on her lip,
Wills silence everywhere.

When Even Cometh On

Lucy Evangeline Tilley

The mother-heart doth yearn at eventide,
And, wheresoe'er the straying ones may roam,
When even cometh on they all fare home.
'Neath feathered sheltering the brood doth hide;
In eager flights the birds wing to their nest,
While happy lambs and children miss the sun,
And to the folds do hurtle one by one,
As night doth gather slowly in the west.
All ye who hurry through life's busy day,
Hark to the greeting that the Ages tell,
"The sun doth rise and set, hail and farewell."
But comfort ye your heart where'er ye stray,
For those who through this little day do roam,
When even cometh on shall all fare home.

*An exquisite sunset over Cape Hatteras National Seashore
paints the Atlantic Ocean near North Carolina's Outer Banks.
Photograph by Terry Donnelly/Donnelly Austin Photography.*

READERS' FORUM

Snapshots from our IDEALS readers

Top left: Ava Crawford, daughter of Mark and Jill Crawford, loves the blanket her great-grandmother made especially for her. Great-grandmother Alma Bickford, of Versailles, Kentucky, shared this snapshot with IDEALS.

Bottom left: Kaycee Joan Babek, nineteen months old, is captivated by her pretty pink bonnet. She is the daughter of Jeff and Jennifer Babek of Clinton, Oklahoma, and the granddaughter of Albert and Betty Babek of Granite Oklahoma.

THANK YOU for sharing your family photographs with IDEALS. We hope to hear from other readers who would like to share snapshots with the IDEALS family. Please include a self-addressed, stamped envelope if you would like the photos returned. Keep your original photographs for safekeeping and send duplicate photos along with your name, address, and telephone number to:

Readers' Forum
IDEALS Publications
535 Metroplex Drive, Suite 250
Nashville, Tennessee 37211

Top:
Ashley Abbott,
daughter of Susan Oliver of Milford, Ohio, and
granddaughter of Dawne Dietz of Cooperstown, New
York, is great friends with distant cousin, Emily
Matuszak, daughter of Tina Haskell of Rotterdam,
New York.

Right: Three sisters, Lizzie,
Danielle, and Madeline,
daughters of Joe and Sue
Raffa, of Castle Rock,
Colorado, show off their
three matching outfits and
their look-alike dolls in dresses
made especially for them by their
grandmother.

Left: Two-year-old Sterling, the
youngest son of David and Ruth
Smith of Arlington, Texas, is ready
for his "noonie" nap with the comfy
blanket made especially for him by
his grandmother, Sue Ford.

Dear Reader,

Enjoying the beauty of spring at the same time as we honor our mothers is appropriate. As we offer lovely flowers and bouquets at the peak of their perfection to those who have guided our lives so unselfishly, we should also be thankful for those gifts of love, compassion, spiritual leadership, and generosity. Our responsibility is, in turn, to share those gifts with others.

Our warmest regards to all those who have raised families and those who are just now experiencing the duties of building a family. May the laughter and joy be as abundant as the beauty of spring.

Marjorie L. Lloyd

ideals

Publisher, Patricia A. Pingry
Editor, Marjorie Lloyd
Designer, Marisa Calvin
Copy Editor, Marie Brown
Permissions Editor, Patsy Jay
Contributing Writers, Lansing Christman, Joan Donaldson, Pamela Kennedy, D. Fran Morley, Lois Winston

ACKNOWLEDGMENTS

BACHER, JUNE MASTERS. "Cradle Quilt" and "I Know a Place" from *The Grandmother Book* by June Masters Bacher. Copyright © 1982. Published by Revell: Baker Book House. Used by permission of George W. Bacher. DICKINSON, EMILY "Nature" from *The Poems of Emily Dickinson*, edited by Ralph W. Franklin, Cambridge, Mass,: The Belknap Press of Harvard University Press, Copyright © 1951, 1955, 1979, 1983 1998 by the President and Fellows of Harvard College. Reprinted by permission of the publishers and the Trustees of Amherst College. JAQUES, EDNA. "To Young Mothers" from *The Golden Road* by Edna Jaques. Copyright © 1953 by Thomas Allen Ltd. Rights returned to Edna Jaques. Used by permission of Louise Bonnell. STIDGER, WILLIAM L. "A Day" from *Poems That Touch the Heart*, compiled by A. L. Alexander. Published by Doubleday. Copyright © 1941, 1956. Used by permission of the author. WILDER, LAURA INGALLS. "Are You Your Children's Confidant? September 1921" from *Little House In the Ozarks*. Copyright © 1991 by editor Stephen W. Hines. Published by Thomas Nelson, Inc. Used by permission of the editor.
Our sincere thanks to the following authors, whom we were unable to locate, for selections that appeared in *Poems That Touch the Heart*, compiled by A. L. Alexander. Published by Doubleday: Homer D' Lettuso for "Old Houses"; Katherine Maurine Haaf for "Good Thoughts"; and W. Dayton Wedgefarth for "Mother's Hands." Our sincere thanks to Wilfrid Charles Thorley, whom we were unable to locate, for "Of a Spider" from his book *The Happy Colt*. We also thank those those authors, or their heirs, some of whom we were unable to locate, who submitted poems or articles to IDEALS for publication. Every possible effort has been made to acknowledge ownership of material used.

Inside back cover: The loveliness of late spring is portrayed in this painting entitled LILAC BLOSSOM AND A BIRD'S NEST, *by Oliver Clare (1853-1927). Image from Fine Art Photographic Library, Ltd., London/Colmore Galleries.*

Left: Lyle and Ronda Krogman of Celina, Ohio, sent this adorable snapshot of their great-granddaughter, Lili, daughter of Matt and Carrie Dase, of Granville, Ohio, in her pink sundress and bonnet.

Go back in time . . . with
Memories of Times Past

Now, in this beautiful book from Ideals, experience wonderful sights, stories, poems, recipes and songs that will stir your soul and take you back to your own *MEMORIES OF TIMES PAST.*

From the moment you open the front cover, you will be transported back to the world of your youth with wonderful stories and poems about family and home, one-room schoolhouses and friends, neighborhood gatherings and parties, with old-fashioned recipes like Mama used to make and pastimes from an age gone by. This beautiful book is illustrated with vintage sepia-tinted photographs, magazine advertisements for products from the past, and exquisite antique rooms.

There are photos and paintings, all with that warm, golden glow of times past. Family stories and poems, some humorous, some tender, all so delightful that you may long for a return to the values of yesteryear.

If you love the past with all of its charm . . . if you love to remember a gentler and slower time . . . if you love the old-time music with its memories . . . and if you enjoy reading the stories and poems of a bygone time . . . you owe it to yourself to take advantage of our offer.

FREE GIFT

Return the Free Examination Certificate today to preview *MEMORIES OF TIMES PAST* for 21-days FREE . . . and receive FREE VINATAGE POSTCARDS just for ordering.

FREE EXAMINATION CERTIFICATE

YES! I'd like to examine *MEMORIES OF TIMES PAST* for 21 days FREE. If after 21 days I am not delighted with it, I may return it and owe nothing. If I decide to keep it, I will be billed $24.95, plus shipping and processing. In either case, the FREE Vintage postcards are mine to keep.

Total copies ordered _____

Please print your name and address:

_____
NAME

_____
ADDRESS   APT#

_____
CITY   STATE   ZIP

Allow 4 weeks for delivery. Orders subject to credit approval.
Send no money now. We will bill you later.
www.IdealsBooks.com   15/202301673

BUSINESS REPLY MAIL
FIRST-CLASS MAIL PERMIT NO. 38 CARMEL NY

POSTAGE WILL BE PAID BY ADDRESSEE

**NO POSTAGE
NECESSARY
IF MAILED
IN THE
UNITED STATES**

**GUIDEPOSTS
PO BOX 797
CARMEL NY 10512-9905**

All FOUR of today's most popular translations of the Holy Bible in ONE magnificent, easy-to-use volume.

Discover new meanings and subtle nuances in Scripture when you compare the majestic and stately words of the King James Version of the Holy Bible with the thought-for-thought approach of the New International Version—or the literal translation of the updated New American Standard Bible with the contemporary-English style of the New Living Translation.

For everyone who loves the power and glory of God's Word...who cherishes each hour spent reading and studying its meanings...who would like to bring greater understanding to a loved one who may be struggling to build a deeper faith. Presented in a clear, easy to read format with complete footnotes, *Today's Parallel Bible* offers Bible readers a way to introduce themselves to different interpretations in their personal search for understanding God's Word.

Save 20% off Publisher's Price

A faith-enriching way to read and understand God's Word!

❧ A 6" x 9" hardcover 2,880 pages of eternal and unchanging truths.

❧ Four popular translations— the King James Version, the New International Version, the New American Standard Bible and the New Living Translation— complete with footnotes.

❧ A unique side-by-side arrangement makes it easy to compare the four translations.

FREE EXAMINATION CERTIFICATE

YES! I'd like to examine *Today's Parallel Bible*, at no risk or obligation. If I decide to keep the book, I will be billed later at the low Guideposts price of only $39.96, payable in 4 installments of $9.99 each, plus shipping and processing. If not completely satisfied, I may return the book within 30 days and owe nothing. The FREE *Magnet Picture Frame* is mine to keep no matter what I decide.

Total copies ordered: _____

Please print your name and address:

_____
NAME

_____
ADDRESS   APT#

_____
CITY   STATE   ZIP

Allow 4 weeks for delivery. Orders subject to credit approval.
Send no money now. We will bill you later.
www.guideposts.org

Printed in USA
11/202301685

We'll send you this colorful Magnet Picture Frame **FREE** when you say "YES!" to our 30-day Free Preview Offer. This brightly patterned magnet pulls apart to form a picture frame—perfect for photos of friends and loved ones—plus, a passage from Scripture to brighten your day!

Free Gift